THE HEAVY-PETTING ZOO

THE
HEAVY-PETTING
ZOO

Clare Pollard

BLOODAXE BOOKS

ISBN: 1 85224 481 X

First published 1998 by
Bloodaxe Books Ltd,
Highgreen,
Tarset,
Northumberland NE48 1RP.

Second impression 2001.

Bloodaxe Books Ltd acknowledges
the financial assistance of Northern Arts.

Cover printing by J. Thomson Colour Printers Ltd, Glasgow.

Printed in Great Britain by
Cromwell Press Ltd, Trowbridge, Wiltshire.

For my family

Acknowledgements

Acknowledgements are due to the editors of the following publications where some of these poems first appeared: *English, Magma, Poetry London Newsletter, Poetry Review, Poetry Wales, The Rialto* and *The Wide Skirt*.

Contents

Nomad

Bury me in desert where sand sweeps
a single magnificent gesture;
where there are no trivialities or
tangles, no sticky knots of feeling

or tear-damp patches, human things.
It is impossible to harm dunes,
or bruise winds, or burn sun.
Desert air is thick with mirage,

so the Bedouin breathe dreams
and move, keep moving, not letting home,
that heavy-hooked numbness, catch them.
And the stars? The stars in the desert

are utterly indifferent to me –
so much so that I think I may fall
in love with stars, those cold-eyed
maps which guide me towards newness.

Do not need me, I need you
to leave my body untended,
my skin naked and unkissed
beneath the dry, valueless gold.

Everything Ends in Ice

The day that I met you
was the first day of sun.
I was shiny and new.
You thawed me in an hour;
made me mute as a flower –
all good clean fun.

As I bit through peach fur
my longing for you grew.
Always knew you loved her,
yet got grazed climbing trees
as you swarmed me like bees.
I sweated you.

Starved of sun, nothing grows,
and rain was all I got.
Watched my dreams decompose,
and lit trees doused in fuel.
You were Halloween-cruel.
You let me rot.

Now, I'm cold as a corpse.
My heart is blank with frost.
Skies are bleak as my thoughts;
and this numbness could slice
as I swallow the ice
and I am lost.

The Heavy-Petting Zoo

It's your best friend's 16th birthday party.
That's eight hamster lives, and yet she still wasn't wise enough
to realise it would turn into a heavy-petting zoo.
Let's put it this way – you wouldn't bring the family,
and there's an awful lot of stroking going on.

The lounge crawls with muzzy, fuzzy pubic mice.
You want to hibernate, but every bedroom is locked.
(That soft-haired girl from the Shetlands is offering rides.)

You could have been a part of it –
for a small price at the door you could have had them
eating out of your hand by now,
felt that breathy, hot nuzzle-lick,
but instead you're floundering in your own sour
vinegar juices, like a sick terrapin.

The other girls are beautiful and brittle chicks,
eggs precarious and smashable in the cups of their bras,
and he's with her somewhere.

They're probably mewling cutely at each other,
or else she's stripped and pink as a piglet
and they're at it like rabbits.
It's sickeningly bestial.
You hope they get myxomatosis.

Yet in your small child's heart you know
that if he'd called you, you'd have followed him as she did.

As a lamb does, whitely and without question.

Zaghruda

I try not to recall the darkest times
for fear that hate will rot away my womb
Khun mae   mon Soeur   daughter
Yes – we touch long desire feel ache also
yet you branded us whores   *huren*

In the brothel the *harem* (skirts up round our thighs)
we lay back and thought of
kuche – centre of our world
jollof rice   dumplings   *bamii nam*   lasagna   *basturma*
At the *suk* we purchased food for you with given coins

sari   izar   veil   tarha
They smothered us   We saw but were not seen
Invisible people devoured by night

I heard of one Asian who killed herself
When you laughed and laughed at the meadows
of soft dark hair on her limbs
We pasted lead on our skin to make us *bleich* for you
You liked us cripples   our feet golden lilies

No ambitions but for you master
whilst you said come on darling   sweetheart   kitten
dog   *querida*   sweet potato pie
In Borneo menstruating women must
sit on the roof for three days

Defloration may involve a sharp stone
or a fist wrapped in cloth
And of course we love the stink of baby crap!
We want to pluck our brows until we weep   *Yed mae*
You sucked our milk then spat it in our faces

The other week Iran was on the news
Men mutilated their own flesh for Islam
At first I cried with joy to see
they had caused themselves to suffer also
Hallelujah!   Fierce *sang rouge* dripping

14

Only then I saw their wounds were as deep as ours
Saw the pained desperate smiles as they tried to be strong
Three men died that day
Oh brother   *padre   sohn*   lover
We anoint your cuts with *yaah saneh* through choice

Forgiveness is easy between equals
Take our hand and we'll love you
Poor sad *Don Juan*
I know we can survive this together

Burn Brighter

Poets construct huge fires
so that God may see them from above.
The tongue is a flame,
and everything fuel for it.

They pile on the rotten, dull, broken,
and pull off charred skeletons of things –
horror burnt off the black bones;
almost bearable.

Sometimes love is a casualty,
caught in white heat, left raw,
its dark sticky skin
too painful to be touched –

but it is worth it for the blast,
the melt, the seconds of brightness.
The poet is an alchemist –
even the most sordid and hopeless hurts

can be licked a scalding gold.
Can combust into a moment
of blistering beauty –
sustenance for these cold months.

The Bridesmaid

I trail behind the bride, watch the dip of the lace
at her waist; a braille I could trace with my thumb.
The bouquets, which smell as the skin at the back
of her neck must, are beautifully done.

Violets for violence. Her gentlest touch
can bruise me, as I cannot stop my blood
from racing to meet her, clamouring to press
against the merest brush of sleeve in a tender flood.

Her ivory straps are biting her back and I long
to slip fingers between her body and them.
I have to clutch hard on the flowers to stop myself reaching,
and slice up my lovesick hands on rose stems.

Roses for the razor she shaved her calves with
this morning; as I watched blossoms she dripped in the sink.
Through steam, as I painted my nails, she talked about love,
how much she was in it, and him, and what did I think?

And the hand which slips a ring on her is not even shaking.
It sickens with anger, this body which has obeyed
love now for a year, which knows every colour her hair
can turn in the light, and is achingly always her maid.

The Butcher's Cat

Butcher, butcher,
                    hack me some meat.
Our poor cat is weak and needs the blood;
for you've drained him, drained him,
neutered and tamed him,
fed him with scraps and with saucers of milk.

Yes, you stroke him with affectionate fingers;
but he saw you SAW that cow
                    in two.

He's seen what you do
to the other animals, butcher-man.
On some hot nights he's watched you tiptoe in
fresh from the slaughter-house –
stinking of iron,
                    an anaemic's wet-dream;
with your blood-drenched boots squealing on the tiles.

He saw the way you fed that hen with best corn,
gave it a name, and then
wrung its neck, as though it had
called your mother a slut.

Butcher, butcher
                    I am sick, real sick
of the obscure cuts you bring me – heart, tongue, sweetmeats;
and that stripey apron that you wear,
and the way you like your steak so rare.
I get MAD when I peer through the grime of your windows
and see the naked limbs –
like fragments of disembodied porn-stars.
                              You pimp death.

And I feel the same fear as our dear pet,
for at night in our big white bed,
stuffed to sickness with sausage;
I have noticed you feel my breast as though
it were a pound of
                           good turkey.
Measuring its leanness.
valuing the meat.

One day soon I will pick up my cat and run,
from you, butcher-man, and your mince. Your stun-gun.
Oh, you say that you would never EAT us –
but I have heard that in France
                           they eat Horse.

Keyf

'I tumble onto my divan and am soon fast asleep,
worn out with the exertion I have not even made.'
HALIDE EDIP

Beside the menagerie,
amongst roses and jasmine
nude women play tag.

Skin is yoghurt,
arms marrows,
breasts eggplants.

A pearl, a ruby –
these things mean nothing.
Are a single

dive through blue
beneath the whetted eye
of a Sultan.

It is the scraps that obsess their hearts –
a match;
a peppercorn;

a slice of pear.
These mean a love that must be silent.
not his sort of love –

a love you share
with those sticky sweet things –
lips of the beauty;

ladies' thighs;
woman's navel.
The ice in their delicate sherbets

has come seventy miles,
and is mixed with pansies, violets.
And is mixed with musk to

20

smother the stink of nothing.
They no more speak truth
than the guard with his slit tongue.

The difference is that their tongues glitter
with crushed lapis lazuli;
pulverised pearl.

Kismet is cured with a little yellow pill.
opiates gild their fates –
it is said those poppies

are white as each face
they blanch with almond paste;
corrode with smoothing arsenic.

And in the end, sisters?
In the end even love ends
with a slice of a scimitar,

or getting stuffed in a sack.
Their veils are an act!
Pretending they have something to hide,

when their lives are
gazing through windows
then bathing off sky.

There's always hope of course.
Did you hear about the eunuch
who found it had grown back?

The magic here is black;
they'd train macaws to cackle lies
to be mistress of robes,

the keeper of the baths.
Each coffee could be poison.
In cliques, they plot their silent war.

Attempt at a Beautiful Poem

I wanted this poem to be beautiful for you.
Longed madly to say pretty things,
but from this café window I can only see
neon shop signs that hum like migraines,
and people sagged beneath them,
                                    hunched from carrying
broken plastic bags full of whisky, beans,
toilet tissue and tinned ravioli.

Those chip-trays could be said to dance like butterflies,
but the bitter milk oozing from crushed dandelions,
however hard I try, can only make me think of pus.

Women tread delicately round dog shit, weeping
black tears for their fetid thighs,
And because *Soldier, Soldier* was so
                                    moving last night.

I could pretend the rain was glistening quicksilver,
but it beats rotting chips to a greasy pulp.
Pummels the man's
                    pasty flesh to bruises
like those on the peaches that roll off market stalls
and decay on the drenched, dark tarmac;

until it would not surprise anyone to see
a maggot squirm out of his shin.

I so wanted to give you a poem that was beautiful,
but somehow I know that promises of
                                    licking you calm
as a sleep-deep ocean, and sap-sticky kisses in forests,
and fists full of stars

are not going to work this time.

Valentine

We always come, dumb with longing.
We come in our thousands –
dressed in pink for shame;

slow-dancing in same-
sex couples.
We are not the broken-hearted –

that's the worst of it.
No excuse but our inadequacy,
as we choke on ginseng, honey,

the stinking truffles
Madame de Pompadour swore by.
Paper hearts flap in the draught.

Body language, rose quartz,
spells, charms, laughing
at every fucking thing that he says…

All false hope,
like the card your mother posts you.
I cannot bear this stench

of tuberose,
pheromones,
fingers.

To want something
is to know I cannot have it.
February leaks its gluey juices;

bleeds over everything.

Dream of Explosions

This is not feverish flamenco fire
devouring my home like a loaf –
this is a margarine candle flame.
Enough light to read by.

This is not a black hole. Nothingness
so intense it thirsts for me –
this is a vacuum flask
full of tea for two.

This is not drowning. Becoming a terrible bird
as the ocean vomits into me –
this is a soothing lukewarm bath
to cure my aching joints.

This is not an earthquake. The world's old wounds
torn open again, like a bad case of scurvy –
this is the peel torn from a tangerine.
A good dose of vitamin C.

I am the cat that got the milk.
Woman who awoke in a warm bed
on a black-ice morning, and never got up again.
My life is nice. I raise a mild smile.

Yes, I dream of explosions
that shake my bones loose,
but what if this is the most violent?
What if this is it, my childhood dream?

I cannot let it go for a whiff of gunpowder.
If I stand in a lonely, open field
trying to catch lightning bolts,
perhaps I'll only catch my death of cold.

Oh, but if I caught that bolt
and sparked the world bulb bright!
Should I settle for this current
that keeps my TV running, but little more?

Angel Song

This fir-tree point could impale.
I balance on it, praying for still skies.
Fingertip bulbs in cracked coloured cases
fuse, and threaten to burn my skirts.

Shiny, red apples decompose on nooses.
Pine cones are sprayed with crunched-mirror glitter.
Sometimes it is thrilling.
This sparkle, this lack of roots.

Only the others hate me. Cry out
that I am no better than them,
it's just my wings are sprayed with gilt
and a halo on a pin skewered through my scalp.

But I earned that jet of golden paint!
I suffered as the pin pierced my soft plastic head,
and unlike them, I cannot make mistakes.
An imperfection and I will be torn from this tree.

I cannot be bitter like a gift of myrrh,
or they'll say: 'Who does she think she is?
Tied to the spike as if it is a crucifixion.'
I am a seasonal decoration,

pretty – but I will not bring salvation.
Tinsel is not real silver, you know,
just foil that moults off strips;
and nobody can join me up here.

What am I but a detail in this small beige room?
An afterthought in an outfit made from
someone's old wedding dress. These needles
bring not sleep, just little hurts.

O, to have a Bethlehem to go to.
To be deep filled, like a mince pie.
Father Christmas, give me wings that work.
I am so tired of trying to rival snowflakes.

Registering Her Complaint

A dream holiday, the brochure said,
but in her dreams the toilet flushes.
She's irritable as a queen
whose gown is made of mosquitoes.
An unripe gecko scurries from her wrath.

The brochure, she is almost sure, did not
inform her it was monsoon season,
the dark trees strung up with liquid fairy-lights,

and though it did not say what sort of breakfast was included,
what sort of breakfast is dribbling chunks of violet melon,
mango, papaya, fresh lychees like turtle eggs?
English people expect an English breakfast –
fat-streaked bacon. Scraping-filled sausages. Tea.

Today she was hoping to lie on the beach,
Aphrodite in nylon knickers, her sweating breasts
strawberry mousses, offending the natives.
Instead they are registering her complaint.

Butterflies huge as bats flap clumsily
past the foyer, as the ceiling fan lazily
thumps the still air. There was a snake
in that bottle of wine, she tells Them,
and in another a rat-foetus – she had nightmares.

The receptionist thinks of his two mud rooms,
the way his daughter begged a biro
off a stranger, and sleeps clutching it.
Arranges for this woman to transfer out of Paradise.

The heat sucks on her like a cigarette.
Her dull eyes dismissing the orchids that are exploding
like invulnerable fireworks in the damp air,
she informs a fellow white there is pressure –
a storm tonight. This at least is something.

Breakfast Poem

I am egg-shell fragile and grapefruit sour.
My face blotchy; eyes raisins soaked in booze.
I stench of night-sweat, am too tired to shower,

to scrub off each ingrained mascara bruise.
Memories slice up my still-sleeping head,
the morning paper does not bring good news.

I'm strawberry-jam sickly; I'm bacon dead.
It's always morning when the ghosts appear –
they haunt my toaster and they burn my bread,

they say I stink as stale as last night's beer.
They laugh with glee to know I burned inside,
once aware that your skin was tasting-near.

I had no resistance; I had no pride.
Confessed my love, then watched you turn to run.
Now my egg tastes salt from tears I've cried,

my soldiers are charred black. No war is won.
I try to weigh my loss against my gain:
I have lost uncertainty, face and sun-

rise. I've gained a hangover; a dull pain.
We're out of milk. My party dress is stained.

A Friday Night at the End of a Millennium

On the first of January
in the year 2000
I will be twenty-one.
Yes, I am a woman

of the next millennium;
star on the clean black.
Our hope for the future.
but I don't give a fuck

as I check my pocket:
purse, lipstick, rape alarm;
and I'm out for the night in a town
where only rain glitters.

Air slits up my wrists
as I head for the pub.
Tottering on thin heels,
a cripple.

We get a seat by the TV screen.
Neck squirming-sour vodka and tonics;
pose with Budweiser bottles.
Soon we are watching *Casualty* with no sound on.

I get cheese and onion crisps.
We gossip to convince our veins
they are not stagnant with boredom.
The room looks like our lounge;

oak beams and a mock-Turkish carpet.
It is full of men who look as though they'd
play dominoes given half a chance.
one winks at me –

And I sneer the sneer of the young and slim.
He could cut his fist on me.
The week's blunt misery
dissolves with the salt off the peanuts.

My mate's called Kerry
and she's game for anything.
Slept with three Ouzo-slick Greeks
on holiday this summer –

sticky one-night stands,
and she's not ashamed.
No, she's proud as can be,
flashing blurred pictures

of her topless. Him fumbling
in his pocket for a spare condom.
At ten we head for the club.
It's symbolically underground.

I order a pint for a pound,
sit on a cracked back chair and begin
to get intoxicated. My ex is here
selling cannabis to pre-pubescent

girls with ultra-bras,
pierced noses, plum hair
and nicotine-gilded fingers.
He is beautiful,

an angel in some lights.
He laughs at everyone,
and is too clever for this world;
fingers greasy with lightly salted puppy fat.

He sweats; snorts vodka
until his nose bleeds prettily.
Laughs some more, then
makes a pass at me on the stairs.

Shit, he is beautiful,
but he only wants me
to prove he gets what he wants –
so I push him away.

The only boy I ever liked to kiss.
It makes me sad but proud.
I have won.
I will learn to live without

his static lips,
the warm dark sparks
that danced softly off his
fingers down my spine.

Dizzy with the punch of winning, I dance.
Jump up and down
like I'm tied to this rotten ceiling with elastic.
I swing my hips,

and lick my lips –
they are dry with cider,
flavoured with salt
and hard-jawed smiles.

I enjoy dancing.
There is a kind of freedom in it,
energy pounding out
of my hunched-up joints.

From the floor I watch
a boy who told me he thinks
I am very attractive –
but he's sleeping with her now.

The big commitment –
get them in bed
and they're caged. Hooked.
Can't wriggle free.

His hair is chilli-red,
his eyes fish scales,
his smile a small boy's.
I used to get giddy when I saw him –

Now I just feel weighted.
Tired. My bones will shatter
like peanut brittle or barley sugar
or some other crap sweet.

Another pint, and they charge
me two pounds this time –
they must have seen me staggering,
but I'm too drunk to care.

Alcohol goes straight through me.
The girls' loos are full
of lads smoking joints,
so I have to piss quietly,

hovering over the bowl
as though I'm a hummingbird
in order to avoid diseases.
Stale urine.

Someone's bloody tampon goads me redly.
I read the sign on the toilet door,
it says: 'AVOID UNWANTED
PREGNANCY – USE A TELEPHONE.'

Oh, that used to make us laugh
when this bitter-dark club seemed new;
when this tongue-moist air
didn't catch in my throat

like a wishbone. I always wish
for something utterly impossible:
lager that hasn't been watered down,
a star, him.

The poor wish fairies –
I am expecting miracles!
It isn't fair on them.
This bad luck is my own responsibility.

It is my own fault,
I take all the blame.
I vow to aim lower and stop thinking
I'm the fucking second coming,

then pull up my silk copping-knickers.
Stumble out, eyes greyed
by a gauze of yeast.
Mirror, mirror on the wall,

says I'm the biggest dog of all.
My flaws glow vivid.
nuclear white light strips my skin off
and leaves the true-me clean.

A regular ugly sister.
Leaves me like a plucked turkey;
face withered and swollen with heat,
lips just a parched outline.

My arms are gorilla hairy in the brightness.
My lip is bald, because I scorched off the hair
before I came out,
with a cream that claimed to be rose

but stank of shit.
My armpits are stubbly jutting caves.
I put deodorant on after shaving
and they stung as though wasps

had built nests in the coves
of dark, moist calcium.
I have a good itch of my bikini line,
readjust my hair – it's sucked sweet sticky.

One lad is trying on his girlfriend's eyeshadow.
Having a good laugh.
It makes me sick-green
to see them crackling with happiness;

to see their reflections –
quivering jelly-fish with hysterics.
He suits it – it is glossy purple,
a pair of artfully blackened eyes.

I watch my nails as I wash my hands.
See I've chipped the *Madly Midnight* polish,
and it sounded so exciting too!
I try to say 'Hi' to someone on the stairs,

only to find my pickled tongue snow-numb.
I cannot speak, mind bleak
as a figureless, hospital-white
winter horizon.

Sitting by the slot machine
that says *Win! Win! Win!*
in the hope its optimism
might rub off,

I listen to
I'm Only Happy When It Rains.
Lose me in empty Diamond White bottles.
Watch others dance,

limbs flying as though
they are epileptic.
All want to pull
but many are too scared.

(What if something falls off?)
Stickily laughing,
I worry about smeared make-up, taxi fares,
my omnipresent virginity – the usual.

Then the inevitable accident –
sweet, sweet cider down
my new blue dress.
I drip like an icicle –

force a smile when a man
in skin-tight army pants
offers to lick it all off
of me for free.

Looking down, I notice
my thighs are exposed.
Our skirts get shorter every week.
My knickers playing hide and seek!

A boy approaches, he is unremarkable,
but at least I feel no nausea.
I may go with him to enhance
my pitiful total of boys kissed so far.

Only I've done that before –
and it leaves me soiled.
The sickening unfamiliarity
of strange tongues;

moist muscle choking you.
A heaving of flesh
with a bruised bud texture
that tastes of vinegar

or, worse, tea-time hot pot.
Dead meat or apples
that have browned for months.
And it either chokes you –

suffocates as though you've
swallowed an Asda bag;
or they're gentle and sloppy –
slobbering dog-like

over your chin, your neck,
your upper lip.
Giving you a wet moustache.
Snail slime slippery

and filling your throat
with its unknown glue-juice
until you want to hide
slug pellets behind your lower teeth.

If you're lucky they'll just
move their tongue in circles –
as though they are drawing
balloons or coins with it.

The monotony dulls your senses
and loosens your jaw.
You want to eat him –
not through lust but

for the thrill of his head in your gullet.
Blood spurting brightly from his warm neck vein,
and you'd swallow it like medicine.
At least then it would be over.

Their stubble grazes your chin,
until it feels as your knees did
when you fell on stony ground as a child.
And if you open your eyes – ugh!

Lids curtain-closed with bliss
as though they're on a train to Paradise,
when you're feeling queasy
and are itching to get free.

Their indignity is distasteful,
their knowledge of your precious mouth.
You want to slap them.
Burn all official records of their being.

Their pleasure and shut-eyed fun is a sick joke –
they think you like them!
It is at times like that
I realise what an ugly word 'snogging' is.

Sometimes, I find myself
Looking around – that's the killer.
Suddenly, you care what everyone thinks;
blush rare-beef pink.

Roast hotly with the realisation
he is not cool, or handsome,
and his character is dubious –
this boy who has his

salivary glands pumping for you.
Who you are sharing spit with.
And you cringe, wince,
try to arrange your hair differently

so nobody will recognise you.
You and this grotesque,
macabre, bladdered freak.
The one with his hands

on your thighs, your back,
the nape of your neck.
He even tries to cop a good
feel up your top –

the nerve of him to think
you are in his league.
On his level.
Not too special to touch.

Anyway, I decide not to go with him.
Laugh for a while as a blond, gay Goliath
licks a hard stripe down
my homophobic male mate's cheek.

My ex reappears,
now vitriolic and revenge-bent;
picks on my sparkly shoes,
and the way I've mislaid my purse.

Flirts violently with
other lager blondes
before my same stale face,
trying to make me cry boozily,

how little he knows me!
I never break,
but am strong as cartilage.
Look, my legs flex as though made of it.

Lights flutter like dying butterflies
in the hot whisky crush.
I am no one, smudged.
A happy blur.

'Are you okay?' someone asks,
and I nod cow-like.
Look at my watch
but see no time, no movement.

Kerry's in the corner
fumbling jumpily with a lad,
legs clenched tightly round him.
People stare a bit, giggling,

then give her a round of applause
when she comes up for air.
She reddens, but not much,
for she loves attention.

Adores a starring role.
Oh, she is a wild-child!
I look shocked, for
it pays to humour her.

See, even drunk I am condescending!
People stomp on my feet.
Rip my tights with careless,
skeletal fingers.

They are trying to destroy me!
I thumb the hole
until it gapes.
A moon made of

lightly downed thigh flesh.
The gold of the hairs shimmers.
Magic dust. Then they
stand erect like little warriors,

and I feel like a hermaphrodite,
and cover it guiltily
as though it is a ripped hymen.
It is cold in here.

So cold I would gasp,
had I the will power
or the energy.
A consuming coldness.

I am a dead foetus
dunked in a lab-jar of ice water.
Exposed and raw,
and I can't feel my pulse,

just the throbbing
of a headache coming on.
Oh, it hurts –
and they've started playing

that terrible Prodigy song.
You know, the one that goes
I've got the remedy, but
only makes me long for Paracetamol.

My stomach churns –
that last pint tipped me over.
My mouth is dry
as a burnt moth.

I perch on the radiator.
Watch my hand clenching
and opening in the darkness.
A sea anemone.

I watch all the people.
The ones who will
dance into the glorious
sunrise with me.

The ones who will kick-start
a new, shining era.
The leaders of men
who will gush like fresh blood

into the next century.
Sacrificial lambs.
The whitest of white;
the brightest flames.

They are joking about blow jobs.
They are inventing nasty
names for one another –
like Trout Eyes.

They are spilling Newcastle Brown
down their Adidas three-stripe tops
and beckoning people
who scare them in broad daylight.

Adjusting spiked hair
and gold hooped eyebrows
in the mirrors of dull
alcoholic lemonade bottles.

And kissing.
Fingering each other's writhing maggot bodies
as though they were cut-glass
or braille or made of flowers.

They are glugging down doubles
with competitive grins.
Shimmying round the shattered shards
of smashed pint mugs

that blossom. An ice web.
They are vomiting a cocktail
of bitter and bile
on the threadbare stairs.

So many people and they all
only want to be loved.
Funny isn't it?
How all could love fiercely

if they only got the chance,
But they won't. It's sad.
Like spilt lager.
Like the taxi ride home.

Surrender

Sometimes you are so raw –
salted eyes crackling; heart bruised to a huge
rotten plum; your back flayed as a galley-slave's –
that you have to stop the slow dance and sit down.

Sometimes you have to accept
that you've been months now underwater,
and no one is going to press their mouth
against your mouth, and halt the airless
agony of your collapsed lungs.

You say you must try, or can't wake and feel alive,
but there are other, quieter ways of living –
some Buddhist monks can so slow down
their hearts that they almost seem dead.
They claim to be content.

Sometimes you have to wave something
white; resisting the temptation to use
a bra, or other underclothes, or
a freshly laundered strait-jacket,
and instead choosing something quite serious:
a square with no yielding curves, cloth
cut from the blanket you bought for the bridal bed.

And that delicious moment when your mind,
muddled from sleeplessness, drink or swelling
caused by beating your desperate head against walls,
desks, the bathroom tiles, thinks for a second,
perhaps maybe they might be possibly yours –
there comes a time when the scars
that cover your body in a web of startling pain
distract you too much for even this to be a pleasure.

There is no redemption, or balm, or daylight.
Sometimes you must just be grateful for a resolution.
Do not look on it as giving up, for there is nothing
to give up. Sometimes the story does end with two people
in separate rooms, and one not even realising this matters.

Light Entertainment

Commissioning a sit-com is
an awful lot of work,
so God created me instead –
what a sadistic jerk!

Right now he's sat in Heaven on
his fluffy white bean-bag,
with cans of beer and kettle-chips,
and probably a fag.

As tears roll down his ancient beard,
his belly shakes with mirth.
He's laughing his huge heart out at
the joke I've been from birth.

Last night a classic episode –
I'd gone to have a wee
when my Dad's friend walks in the room.
There goes my dignity!

I spilt my drink, I burnt the eggs,
I picked up a verruca.
Forgot to set the video
for *Friends*, and lost at snooker.

And what great comic timing then
to hit me with love's darts!
I thought perhaps my luck had changed –
forgot that stooge, my heart.

That stale old joke: I fail with bloke!
This show has lost its spark.
These same sick gags are wearing thin.
God's humour's just too dark.

Bangkok

Thousands of monks
like burning clementines
heads smooth and shiny
as mud puddles.

Thousands of male tarts,
slender and painted –
with eyelashes
to make me envious.

Thousands of people on
bicycles. Tricycles.
Mopeds and tuk-tuks.
Cars and taxis.
Riding on elephants.
Travelling by foot.

Pouring out of incense-heavy buildings
like a fleshy discharge.
Clotting up the crossroads
and the junctions like scabs.

Even on the murky mushroom river
with its glorious stink,
they pile onto the ferry boats
until they look like they will sink.
Heaving. Breathing.
Yards of skin that smells of lemongrass.

Once, led past the small, hot stalls –
full of steaming satay and coconut milk –
I was taken to a temple made
of marble, gold and jade;
within which, in sticky coolness,
they laid deep pink lotus flowers,
uniform as folded linen napkins
at the altar as gifts.

Smiling, our guide said:
'There are no individuals in this world.
We are all part of the same great spirit.
When you can accept this and become part of everything –
then you will reach Nirvana.'

But I screamed: 'No!
I am an individual.
No one else thinks these thoughts I have.
Nobody looks just like I look.
Separate and removed – I am no part of you!
I am special.
I am different.
I am me! Me! Me!'

Apparently, I fainted then.
They brought me round with tiger-balm
and curries so hot I wept,
but their kindness no longer seemed so selfless.

Drug-happy on the morphine
of Buddha's fat smile,
they did not understand when
I begged for solitude.

When I told them I would rather be
the only orchid in this city,
than a wet, pink cell
inside the cheek of a goddess.

Losing Control

The bank is all sluggish veined marble,
silence and grandeur, a horrible church.

'Are you saying your cash-card is stolen?'
Eyes grey as incinerated five-pound notes
gaze on me in disappointment. 'No, lost,'
I confess, a sinner, through the glass.

It seems I lose everything these days –
keys, dignity, pool games, nerve,
the ring my Grandmother left me.

The staff are bowed and hushed before
computer screens as though in prayer.
I am passive as a two pence piece, passed
around, dull from fingers. I have lost

control. Hunched over the toilet
as though sheltering from a holocaust,
I dribbled sick, that sweet yolk,
down my chin and blouse last night.

'Name?' My dry lips clamp on absence.
Footsteps are gunshots through pillows.
I am suddenly six again, bawling
redly, alone in the supermarket.

And the people who are queuing to receive
coins like communion wafers, stare greedily.
'Name?' Through hallowed quiet her voice
echoes like the tannoy did that day:

'We have a small, frightened blonde girl
here, can someone please come to claim her...'

Still Life

I have taken up painting since I fell in love with you,
as my hands are quite desperate for something to do.

Still lifes mainly, as it makes me impossibly grateful
to gaze on something beautiful until my eyes are full –

you always run from me whilst I'm still hungry to stare.
It's a common misconception that there's just fruit there;

no, my canvases are laden with longing and lust.
Desire aches a gloss of sweat into the oil-paint crust.

At first, plums were nipples full of gold milk; ripe and ready,
my apples were firm and smooth, that heady

fertiliser taste clutching their skin, sour and strong –
as chemical as my make-up would taste to your tongue.

Oranges promised a sharp, delicious bite
and then juice gushing out like a cry in the night.

When you started dating her I drew spat-out pips,
the poisonous berries that grew around her hips.

I daubed maggots in the core of each pink cherry,
they squirmed out from the heart of every strawberry.

In art class I was told I'd lost all sense of perspective;
my slit-split skinned pears were no longer objective.

I stopped sleeping, began to sit up all night and paint
my fetid black bananas, melons swollen and faint,

and those peeled grapes, silver as your blind eyes.
Are you allergic? Am I crawling with fruit fly?

Without even tasting me, how is it fair to refuse?
Did nobody tell you that once you've inflicted a bruise,

all the flesh around the hurt goes rotten brown?

Delay

Businessmen are eating pre-packed sandwiches;
they smile, as though aware
I can't really afford the fare to London.
My face is licked on the pane with a milky tongue.

The anaemic countenance
haunts rivers, office-blocks, mills –
ghost of those who drowned internally,
damning up dreams until canals

of stagnant water carried their corpses
out of those industrial towns.
On one eye is a statue of Mary and child;
on one eye is a supermarket;

her tongue is weighted with
a cathedral,
a town hall;
her mouth is the scar of a derelict road

glittering with wasted streetlights.
They never apologised for the delay;
although inside she screamed like
the brakes when they said

You must disembark, miss, the line goes no further.
My reflection moistens her lips, my lips,
ready to bite down on some city, to tear it
with our teeth, and swallow it entirely.

Butterfly Collector

The lake skin was the skin
of a corpse, grazed by the wind,

and the rank grasses caressed his shins,
juices bleeding and soaking.

He observed butterflies,
those gaudy Icari,
dumbly fluttering.
Vowed to protect them from the drip-drip,
the terrible dark plunge.

The first that he caught was a Painted Lady,
her tawny orange silks convulsing beneath
his thick-fingered hand, spasms melting to calm.

Later, he learnt to make a net from nylon
curtain fabric, a hoop from clothes line.
Used ammonia to poison
softly as backhanded compliments.

Recently he has been murdering the rainbow –
he has a Red Admiral,
an Orange Tip,
a Green Hairstreak.

Desperately, he aches for the Pale Clouded Yellow;
dreams every night of its buttery wings
beating against his face like eyelashes.

It is still the painted lady he adores though.

He didn't mean to break her antennae that time.
Stuck them back on with a tear-drop
of seccotine applied to the head.
You wouldn't know there'd been any damage.

Even at work, he finds himself imagining
they are in some garden together.

He is an Adonis Blue.
The flutter of her wings
mirrors his heart.

Some days he plucks out the setting needle,
gestures for her to fly, free, luxuriating
in his own benevolence. She does not move.

The caterpillars writhe amongst thistles, nettles,
their flesh breeding dark hairs like pubis.

Each time the needle plunges back in deeper.

Poem for My Future Love

I do not want a settle for second-best love.
A mundane grow-to-love-him
cosy little rut love.
A pizza and a video,
holding hands and making plans romance.
I do not want to be able to look at him without crying.
I do not want to be able to eat in his presence.
I do not want to be fond of his little ways
or to have fun whenever he's not there.
I do not want our meeting to be a cute
anecdote to tell our children,
or to buy him aftershave for Christmas
and receive French knickers in return.
To go to the cinema with him and kiss
mildly on the second to back row.
I do not want to fall in love by halves.
A dilute Milk Tray
and two dozen red roses love.
A maybe-this-is-it
slow dancing and fancying romance.

I want to fall in love so hard it bruises.
I want to fall in love so hard it scars.
I want to fall in love so hard it fractures,
and cuts my knees and slices up my arms.
I want to fall in love so badly I cough up blood.
So madly I would confess to murder.
So terribly I would gouge out my eyes.
So painfully I would gas myself.
So utterly I would eat mud and bone.
So crazily I would leap off
ten-storey buildings in the night.
I want a love that chokes me. Blinds me.
Stabs me. Shoots me. Rips and burns me.
Tears and wounds me.
Heals me like new skin.

It will be a passionate stupid vengeful
breathless arrogant tender devouring
painful fiery dirty gentle fumbling
vicious beautiful glittering fatal
pure love.
It will be a complete and utter whole and total
everything and all love.
A love that is blind to colour.
A love that is deaf to warnings.
A love that does not feel the cold.
A love that does not taste the blood.
Not the kind of love
you learn to take for granted,
but the kind of love that makes you live in fear,
and feel like you're only living when he's near.
A love that will make breathing seem trivial.
That will make time stop dead
and the sun burn out.

When he touches me my skin will sing.
I will become electrically charged.
I will tremble and ache when he speaks.
I will smile stupidly at his name.
I will start crying for no reason.
I will love the smell of his limbs
and the taste of his tears
and the sweep of the curve of his back
and the rhythm of his heart
and the patterns of the pale blue veins on his wrists.
I will only be able to sleep when he is holding me.
I will talk to him even when he is not there.
I will kiss him so hard my mouth will bleed.
I will hold him so hard even surgeons will
not be able to separate us,
and for so long we will turn to
ash and crumble.
I will love him so much it will be illegal.
Dangerous.
I might explode.

I do not want a settle for second-best love.
A mundane grow-to-love-him
cosy little rut love.
a pizza and a video
holding hands and making plans romance.
I am waiting for the love that will renew me
and send electric currents screaming through me.
When I fall in love there will be
thunder. Lightning. Fireworks.
I am waiting for the love that I deserve.

Fresher

It was to be a whole new chapter
in the grim little pamphlet of his life.
David became Dave, owner of Diesel jeans and obedient hair.
His record collection was pared down brutally.

He had anticipated girls with nipples
big as the bottoms of beer-bottles.
Their smiles white as vacant signs on toilet cubicles.
There would be drunken sex on someone else's beanbags,
Sneaking from curry-houses stinking of unpaid-for vindaloo,
blowing each day's budget on lager and a twenty deck.
He'd make mates who could supply him with quality gear,
scrape illicit powders to lines with his student union card.

Yet here he is, in his bedroom at half past one,
soberly wanking to distant techno beats,
a stale taste in his mouth. His head swims
with the short girl from geography who blanks him.

And lying by the papery wall that his groans
of reciprocated pleasure were to cause disturbance through,
he can hear someone pissing. Nothing is new.
It is all just the same but more impersonal.

Hara-kiri

It is as small, complex and compact
as a microchip.
(God must be Japanese.)

They will hook it out limb by limb.
Tough veined trout pink flesh
as raw as sushi.

Nothing will remain of it but
bloodspots on her bright white sheets
like stubborn flags.

If she let this grow it would
cripple both of them.
Hearts mutated by the fall-out.

It would want to die for her.
Kamikaze pilot.
A noble death.

It's karaoke!
Everybody in the ward sing:
'Baby, where did our love go?'

Career prospects and finances and practicality
are squatting like sumos on her mind,
and this rising sun holds no promise,

for she will attack at herself at dawn
and there will be
no surrender.

She will slit herself open.
Watch it and her intestines slip out
in the light of a Samurai sword.

The Last Love Poem

1

This is the last love poem,
there will be no more.

*I charge you, O daughters of Jerusalem, if ye find
my beloved, that ye tell him, that I am sick of love.*

For two years, a doll of you rattled round
my scratched, spluttering heart chambers.
Last night I tore it out,
wiped off the gunk, the bloody slobbers,
found the petty limbs shoddily made.
Did I say your eyes were kind skies?
They were painted sticky chlorine.
Did I call your mouth perfection?
It was just a splintered jut,
moles nestling below it like rooks.

I take everything back.

2

Love *n.* warm affection; sexual passion;
wholehearted liking for something; beloved person.

It was 2 a.m. on their first date.
He took her to the derelict hospital,
its gutted wing was rain drenched; incurable.

And she always knew he would never be her suitor,
her *cavaliere, wooer, amoroso,* his tongue
ugly malt-sticky with Marlboro Lights,
that thick Bolton accent pronouncing *affaire
de cœur,* grande passion, made her laugh.

But oh, the way he jerked from her touch,
as though she'd tried to slip ice-cubes
down his shirt, hurt like she was chewed up,
bitten, smitten, spoony, her gut spooned out.

3

*The more you arch, the more access he has to your breasts
and clitoris, and by being on top you have total control
over how fast and how hard you want to go.*

*If ever any beauty I did see,
which I desir'd, and got, t'was but a dreame of thee.*

The club flickers with the peach light of skin
feigning arousal, the screens show thighs, ill-
fitting uniforms, cheap off-white lace, bodies
writhing in slicks of oil, like dying birds.
She drinks the cocktails. *Long slow screw.*
Multiple orgasm. Slippery nipple. The creamy
green *Shag.* They are embarrassing to ask for,

but she does, though her shy tongue
would not dare articulate her real thirst.
*There is a scar on Beth's forehead,
a small indentation made scratching at chicken-pox.
I want to give her everything.*

Pamela Anderson fucks on a motorbike.

4

*Here love his golden shafts employs, here lights
his constant lamp and waves his purple wings,*

Did I say how nice your mouth was? Did I say?
There's something wrong, isn't there? Tell me what's wrong.

These, lulled by nightingales, embracing slept,
And on their naked limbs the flowery roof showered roses.

There's something wrong. I'm paranoid, forgive me.
Do you still love her? Tell me. There's something wrong.

Know to know no more.

5

Love was invented by the church
to encourage monogamy and reduce illegitimate births.
Love was invented by the capitalists
to ensure a system of patrilineal inheritance.
Are you listening?
It is a fake, whatever the hell you think you're feeling.
It is socialisation, and Wonderbra adverts,
and biological practicality, and the ruling elite.
In most countries romance doesn't even exist.
It's a big western lie.
IT IS IN YOUR FUCKING HEAD.

Some people say they are in love every week,
some never say it, some say it once (but afterwards,
finding red-eyed photographs or weeping over sliced
onions, feel nothing but impotence), some feminists
feel *in love* is impossible in our oppressive society,
some girls buy magazines for the front-page promises:
how to catch your man, twenty ways to make him love you,
some people will not change for love, some cannot,
some look in the mirror and do not recognise their own
breasts, or necks, kissed to cream and purring.

Baby's good to me, you know, she's happy as can be,
you know, she said so.

Ironic, how the moon looks like a contraceptive pill.
How love drenches the loved, whilst the loveless
suck at the stems of roses, hoping for moisture,
slicing up their mouths on the barbed wire stems.

Am I bent?
Yes.
Will I ever be happy?

6

Certain words belong in love poems:
milk, sweat, swallow, cinnamon,
jasmine, hummingbird, indigo,
nectarine, salt, humid, cut.
They mean nothing, but he likes
to watch her mouth shape the sounds:
scar, molasses, beloved person.

7

...And to win tonight's big prize of eternal misery,
you simply have to complete the sentence: Love is..
a) When you cannot see any flaws, or
b) When you see all the flaws, and love each utterly.
Answer it incorrectly,
and you're suffering for NOTHING, you stupid bitch!

Lucy loves Chris loves Sarah
loves Karen loves John loves Anna.

This worm eats heart-flesh,
tongue-flesh, thigh-flesh.
It is in the drinking water,
the bedclothes, the loo-roll.
WAKE UP!   IT WILL EAT YOU ALIVE!
RUN!   HIDE!

Anna loves Steve loves Kate
loves Matt loves Tom loves Louise.

This worm eats eye-jelly,
ear-drums, crotch-meat.
It is in your Beatles albums,
your TV, your stockings.
DON'T LOOK!   IT WILL LEAVE YOU FOR BLIND!
RUN!   HIDE!

Lovelorn *adj.* forsaken by or pining for a lover.
Comfort me with apples: for I am sick of love.

8

In 1995, approximately 40 percent
of marriages were found to end in divorce.

Her love altered where it alteration found,
so was not love, merely infatuation, a crush.
But oh my God she was crushed utterly,
and who can claim to know how love is measured?
She cried into the bathroom carpet all
Christmas Day for that man, and did not
count the tears, but the wool was sodden.
Her face took the texture of the weave.

(Oh, but he will suffer, she tells herself.
One day he will wake to find that loss has
kidnapped him, and he is gagged and bound
in a dark, rat-ridden cellar. One day
he will realise the scale of her worth
and, awestruck, hack off those fingers
which allowed her to slip through.)

To know know know him is to love love love him
and I do.

59

9

By night on my bed I sought him whom my soul loveth:
I sought him, but I found him not.

In your room, with its stained duvet, your
Che Guevara poster, the guitar which clings
jealously to your fingerprints, do you dream
about me ever, do you wake up touching yourself,
the breeze flickering against your skin
like my eyelashes, seeing ghosts of my hair,
my hip bones bruising your eyelids?

Last night, every night, I dream of you.

I dreamt I saw you across the still lake,
and screamed at you for giving me this burden,
this melancholy, this rotting smell.
You looked up, your face a torn petal
against the ache of the dark forest,
and we two stood staring at each-other,
my arms laden with feathers, flesh,
and the stones which weighted me,
a paper doll, to your awful silence.

10

Ev'ry time we say goodbye, I cry a little.

How the world was made, the afterlife,
infinity, the soul, all the great questions
mean nothing, nothing at all, when she is close
and can almost lick the raw, bitten down skin
where he tore the fingernail off with his teeth.

Whitethroat, skylark, goldfinch, they dip
and soar, quite loveless, yet still alive.
How can they not sink beneath the weight of
no breath on skin, no tongue, no *I love you*, ever?

11

Did my heart love till now? Forswear it sight!

So that is it? Just friends? I cannot bear it.

For I ne'er saw true beauty till this night.

Can't you see what you are doing? You will destroy me.

Thus from my lips by thine my sin is purged.

Talk to me. Say something. You will destroy me.

Give me my sin again.

Shantih, shantih.
Oh, but his mouth is the most beautiful thing.

12

This was to be the last love poem,
but I love him, and if I say it enough he might love me.

I will write other love poems –
It is fucking degrading.

Stars I have named after him
grind into my skin like crushed glass.